DEAR NKWERRE

poems by

NGOZI OLIVIA OSUOHA

TRANSCENDENT ZERO PRESS

HOUSTON, TEXAS

PUBLISHED BY TRANSCENDENT ZERO PRESS
www.transcendentzeropress.org

ISBN-13: 9781946460295
Library of Congress Control Number: 2020951899

Printed in the United States of America

Transcendent Zero Press
16429 El Camino Real Apt. #7
Houston, TX 77062

Cover design by: Opara Barnabas Chidiebere,
Musterseed Computers

4B OYIMA STREET,
OWERRI, IMO STATE,
NIGERIA,
WEST AFRICA.

FIRST EDITION

DEAR NKWERRE

poems by

NGOZI OLIVIA OSUOHA

BOOKS BY THE AUTHOR

The Transformation Train
Letter To My Unborn
Sensation
Tropical Escape (Co-Write with Amos O. O'jwang)
Fruits From The Poetry Planet
Poetic Grenade
Whispers Of The Biafran Skeleton
Freeborn
Raindrops
Chains
Eclipse Of Tides
The Subterfuge
Green Snake On A Green Grass
Chariots Of Archangels
Interwoven
Wonderment
The Phenomenal Human
Xenophobicracy
Destiny
Suicide
Christmas Fever
The Rhythm Of Life

Table of Contents

MAY IT NEVER BE TOLD

Dear Nkwerre, I am so troubled that I cannot speak. The chronicling dilemma and the traumatizing drama tear me up and wing me apart. Power and Might muscle me down and the tussle ravage my spirit.

Dear Nkwerre, may it never be told that your giants made you a dwarf.
May it never be written that your stakeholders burned your stake.
May it never be said that your dancers went lame on stage.
And may it never be read that your legends crippled your future.

Mother, my native land, may it never be heard that your warriors butchered themselves.
May it never occur that your knights in shinning armour sheath their swords against intruders.
O my dear elephant, may vultures never feast on your carcass.
Dear motherland, may it never be told that your sons severed sonship.

Dear Nkwerre, may it not be in record that your Irokos uprooted you.
Far be it from history that your miners planted landmines.
May it never be on chronicles that gold diggers dug your grave.

My dear native home, may spectators and passersby never spit on you.
May history never allow your soldiers invade your camp.
May your gurus never fan war nor your geniuses sow hate.

Dear Nkwerre, may it never be told that your nobles disgraced you.
May it be unheard that your pride and dignity should be dented.
May the kindred spirit never be mortgaged.

These drawn swords hurt the dead, frustrate the living and limit the unborn.
Let it not be told that your custodians customized curses.
May it never be said that your titled men truncated your traditions.
Never it be sung that your corridors castrated your cultures.
May your chamberlains never pull you down.

Let rivalry and superiority not shatter your foundations,
May supremacy and quest not trigger your destruction,
For selfishness and greed can only feed the weed.

Motherland, may your fields not be barren
May strangers never plough your lands
May your waters never turn bloody and bitter,
Mama, may your roof never be burnt by your patriots and
philanthropists.

Nkwerre Imenyi, may politics never cripple the sacrifices of your
ancestors.
May your passion for freedom not land you into slavery.
May your vision not be blurry
May it never be told in the house of your enemies that your gods raped
your virgins.
May your friends never betray you,
And may your ignorance not multiply your dangers.

Dear Nkwerre Opiaegbe, may we never tell our children that we aided
your downfall.
May it never be found in the archives how we poisoned your porridge
or sold our birthright.
May no exodus chronicle lamentations.

May it never be told at the marketsquare that your wrestlers were
defeated by women.

Dear Native Land, may you not be the white chick that gave itself to
the hawk,
May you never be likened to the "indestructible" Titanic which later
became a monumental tragedy.
Fervently do I pray, earnestly do I hope, that this mighty scourge of
war may speedily pass over us.

Dear Nkwerre, strengthen your sons
Shield, protect and guide them
Let there be peace and harmony
May they be in one accord,
Fortify them against external forces
Bless them beyond measure
Restore and continue to restore their dignity
Keep them at ease that things never fall apart.

THIS AMBITION IS NOT WORTH OUR BLOOD

Our craftsmen have gone home
Let them rest in peace,
Our blacksmiths have fallen asleep
Do not disturb their rest,
We need no gun.

Peace is our incense
Progress is our success,
Love is our move
Dove can it, prove;
We need no gun.

This is our stool
If we make it a school
People will learn and be no fool
If we make it a pool
They will swim and be cool,
But if we make it a war-tool
We may become like the cotton wool.

Unity is our identity
Security is our responsibility
Integrity is our charity,
Necessity is our priority
Ability is our audacity.

O my beloved brethren
Men of timber and calibre
The Irokos and giants of our dear Nkwerre
This ambition is not worth our blood.

Prestige is our heritage
Ego is our logo
Pride is our stride,
We teach others to learn.

Dream is our beam
Hope is our rope,
Dedication is our foundation

Revival is our survival,
We need no gun.

We learn to teach others
Ponder anew, look yonder,
If this ambition is worth our blood.

They said Ajinmiri saved Nkwerre during the Biafran War
These war drums we beat
These war songs we chant,
These war gongs we carve
This Surugede we dance,
Need I remind us that Ajinmiri is no more?

Imenyi! Opiaegbe!!
Ogara Mba di ugwu,
Ihe onye shiri ya zere.

A NOBILITY IN CAPTIVITY

This is our paternity
And our maternity;
To us, it means sanctity
In every bit of formality
And sense of normality,
Our dear nativity
Is a clarity
And the authenticity
Of our authority,
It is a certainty
And a duty
With great opportunity
To serve the society;
A clear responsibility
To provide amenity
For the profitability
Of our community,
Hence we need tranquility
From each personality
Whether or not a celebrity
For great productivity.
In this curiosity
We must avoid casualty
Because all is vanity
No matter the vicinity,
Therefore in sincerity
Let us unleash credibility
In our speciality,
For us to have the capability
And the capacity
To tackle any eventuality
In our locality
As we lean on flexibility.

For our versatility
Is already a university
No matter the adversity,
Therefore let this polity;
A blessed fraternity
Focus not on futility
Lest it becomes a Nobility In Captivity.

THIS RAGING SEA

Hush! Hear the marine kingdom sing
Lo, watch the mermaids dance
See, the feast and the banquet is ready
This raging sea is ungodly.

Hear the sea echo in anger
And the waves rock in passion,
Tides rolling back and forth
Times ticking round the clock,
Storms spin and giggle in force
The violent sea in anticlockwise.

Ripples of the raging sea
Splash across homes and hearts
In loud noises of fear and doubt
With lightning and thunder
Moaning hard and groaning deep
Warning against a heavy rain!

Reverberations and incantations
Enchantments and divinations
Hunting calmness and tranquility
Foiling happiness and unity,
Pushing daggers, pulling swords
Drawing lines, stroking poles
O what a godless sea!

Turbulent waters, roaring sea
Seductive mermaids, poisonous demons
O this shipwreck is avoidable!

Dust; ill-winds and whirlwinds
Disasters; manmade and natural
Maze; web, networks and links
Interwoven; tetra, hydra, ultra, intra, extra
This raging sea is callous!

See the weak hands of the unborn
Feel the feeble knees of the living,
O hear the troubled breasts of the dead
Fearing this ship may sink after all.

But tell captured hearts of our vanquished
The territorial maps of our conquests
That this ship is sailing farther.

Strong souls of our forefathers
Lovely spirits of our ancestors
Footprints of our deities
Seductive voices of our goddesses
Do not watch this sea, rage!

Green land of mighty men
Rich waters of powerful folks
Serene air of true heroes
Soothing breeze of peaceful legends,
Listen, we dare not sink!

You silly raging sea
We anchor, we swim, we dive, we float;
Freestyle, breaststroke, backstroke
We are current, we are synchronized,
Peace! Be still!!

TWINKLE TWINKLE MOTHERLAND

Twinkle, twinkle, motherland
How your wonder warms my heart,
Just a puzzle hard to solve
Like a mystery beyond my scope.

Twinkle, twinkle, beautiful star
You enlighten great and far,
With your head above the bar
You are made; let nothing mar.

Twinkle, twinkle, motherland
For you, is the Seraph band,
Inscribe your name not on the sand
For God has you on palm and hand.

In dark tunnels, you race in hope
Moving across lands and climes,
Twinkling for generations yet unborn
Praying for uncommon dawn.

Motherland of diverse gifts
Heroine of unique beauty,
Goddess of plenty talents
Empty not yourself in want.

Twinkle, sparkle, dazzle, shine
Tickle, tangle, buckle, dine
Sing, dance, run, play, wine
Till your fears fall into line.

Twinkle, O gracious mother
Breastfeed us glorious motherland,
Unite us, O blessed nature
Secure us courageous motherland.

Twinkle from our footwears
Twinkle upon our footsteps
Twinkle around our footpaths
Twinkle in our footmarks,

Twinkle through our footprints
Twinkle, twinkling, our footstools.

High, higher, Opiaegbe
How I wonder how you fly,
Up above the world so high
Like an eagle in the sky.

PASS THROUGH THIS LAND

Pass through this land
Kindle its glow again,
Ignite its passion once more
That those in Babylon, strand
May know trouble is vain
And see lust as sore.

May our hairs not fill our pores
No matter the magnitude of scores,
Go yonder us and before
Refine our every ore
Dig to the core
Lord, pass through this land.

Lord, pass through this land
Erase all its pain
And enlarge its store
That those who build on sand
May learn the dangers of rain,
And know it can anything, gore.

Lord, pass through this land
Make it rich and plain
Let there be unity galore
That those who seduce its band
May understand the stain
And put away their whore.

Lord, pass through this land
Teach us to care
And not to sow any tare
Help us firm, to stand
That we know our worth
Rather than go back and forth.

Pass through this land, dear Lord
Break bows and arrows
Feed men and sparrows
And sheath their sword,
Descend, that they transcend
Ascend, that they blend.

Keep us safe from danger
Protect this our manger
Ward off every evil stranger
On this land, dear lord, focus
Give us peace, unity and locus
That we appreciate the bonus,
Pass through this land through us.

Quicken our mortal body
That we, be not moody
Save us from this muddy water.
Lord, rebuild our tents
Let your angels be the agents
Please make it a celestial matter.

This train, lead, merciful light
Preserve every soul, compassionate Being
Water each grain, enliven the seed
In this journey, thyself delight
Grant this boat, a smooth sailing
Driver, pilot, captain, to us heed.

Shine upon our homeward way
Purge our land of this scourge
Encourage us in every stage
Manage our lot in each age,
Stay with us; miry clay
Lay with us that we do not stray
Keep our fainting heart to not weep
Way; our homeward, thyself steadily shine.

IT IS NOT A MESS

The day is cloudy
And the night, moody
The land is flooded
And the air bombarded,
Hearts are stony
And spirits, thorny.

We betray at will
And willingly stray,
We get our fill
And fling the stay,
We pay the day to have our way
We grill, bill and chill
Chilling at the windmill.

We invoke the hill
And yet remain still,
We can neither till nor drill
Because we choke from the smoke
So we stroke the spoke,
And then become so woke
That we cannot joke.

We turn wool to coal
And burn out our goal,
Then we sell the field
To buy a shield,
What we always bargain
Is nothing but our gain.

A loose hand of fate
Pulling down our gate,
Nurturing and harbouring hate
Watering anger at a high rate,
Planting disarray beyond date.

We force the horse to the stream
Just to fulfill our dream,
We kill the dog along the way
And have our pay,
We march on brass
Just to show our class,
Then shatter the glass
To have our pass,
We play on, with the chess
And still prove It Is Not A Mess.

IF YOU SEE MY UNBORN

If you see my unborn
Teach him to be humble
That life is a jungle,
It can burst like a bubble
And can anyone, crumble
So if he must grumble
Let it not be from gamble
Because even a pebble
Can kill the great and noble
If they do wobble.

If you see my unborn
Teach him to avoid trouble
Because it can make him stumble
Even if he can wrestle,
They may boil him in kettle
And make his knees feeble.

If you see my unborn
Teach him to not be arrogant
No matter how buoyant
For everyone is important,
Because as big as the elephant
He cannot stop the ant.

If you see my unborn
Tell him to not sell his pant
Because waters, be they stagnant
Can kill especially the ignorant
And human, be he, infant
Has his psalm to chant,
So let him not always rant
For everything he would want.

If you see my unborn
Teach him to tame his horn
He must not act nude or porn
Just to have some corn,
For whatever he would have worn

In a minute, can be torn
Even in the morn
And that would be his thorn.

If you see my unborn
Teach him to be a cook
Rather than a crook,
Teach him to be a farmer
Instead of a charmer
Help him be a teacher
Rather than a cheater.

If you see my unborn
Never let him be a clown
So that I would not frown,
If you see my unborn
Please do not let him drown,
Rather teach him to sew his gown
Be it blue or brown.

If you see my unborn
Please do not let me down,
Teach him he must not wear a crown
For him to build his town.

MY NEWEST HYMN, TUNED AFTER "ABIDE WITH ME"

Sprinkle thy blood around this weary earth
Twinkle the glow that chases ill and death,
Kindle the love that binds in peace and joy
Battle the force that may rise to destroy.

Upon our face, mark thyself and thy grace
Button thy mace on those who run the race,
Torn, though their lace, endue them at thy pace
Won their place, blessed; all those who scored the brace.

Nothing does last, not even from the blast
Though high like mast, all changes even fast
Let us cast all our pain and all our past
Upon the Cross that we may bear no loss.

In one accord, let us sheath every sword
Within; we shall lord, without and forward
Sin untoward, for no more a coward
Win trouble, pain, shame, and not step backward.

Abide here Lord, dwell beyond far and wide
Hide not thy face from ocean's time and tide,
Divide her not, for she is thy dear bride
Confide in her that she turns out, thy pride.

Above the pain of sabotage and self
Move thy hand quickly to rescue thy dove,
Shelf not thy peace, not even thy pure love
Prove to the whirlwind of thy whole true self.

Bring thy mercy, spread it on every wing
Cling thyself to us, that we clean the ring,
Sting us not lord, let nothing do us, fling
Sing, we shall always do to thee, great King.
(Dedicated To Nkwerre)

DEAR MAMA

Wonders shall never end. Sometimes, forces of destiny negate comprehension and the mysteries of fate compound wonderment.

So unfathomable, Dear Mama.
Look mother, the foetuses you almost died while carrying now say you are barren and impotent.

The pregnancies you bore, now teach you pushing and childbearing.

The babies you sang lullabies to put to sleep now want you in coma.

The children you breastfed now say you no longer have breasts.
And the ones you christened now call you pagan.

Dear Mama, even the children you delivered while working in the farm, now call you lazy.
The children you carried up the mountain to fetch water and quench their thirst now say you are a powerless wilderness.
Those you bore down the valley to gather firewood now call you a witch.

See the ones you gave revelations now rebel against you, the children you told stories, fairy tales, chronicles, folklores, and secrets, under the moonlight, now teach you history.

Dear Mama, see the ones you built international colleges for, and chased them to school with cane, now call you illiterate.

Look at the ones you hid in trenches, bushes, backyards and inside barns, during the war, for their safety and also for them not to be conscripted, they now weld weapons at you.

The toddlers you sucked their nostrils, those that urinated and defecated on you now say you are dirty and stinking.

See the babies that never allowed your succulent breasts to rest even in public, now call them sour and saggy.
Even those you tore your Hollandis wrappers to pack their vomits and excreta at occasions now say you are naked and wretched.

24

The infants you woke up at cockcrow, backed and trekked to Nkwo, Eke, Orie, and Afor, to buy and sell, in order to pay their fees and bills, now want to buy and sell you.

Even the ones you preserved breastmilk for, in coconut shells, now want to axe you.

The children you warmed around your tripod stand under your leaking thatched hut have built heavens and paradise, so now they want to send you packing.

Dear Mama, look at the ones you pumped their anus and dressed their circumcision, they have come to attack you.

Also, the ones you sent to the west have returned to westernize you.

The very ones you taught celibacy have been seduced to rape you.

Dear Mama; meek and gentle, loving and caring, please forgive them for they know not what they do.
Teach them that life is vanity upon vanity. Shine your light and open their eyes.

Dear Mama, pass through the strangest stony heart, for all the hearts of men are in your care.

THE DIGNITY OF OUR IDENTITY

Dear force of gravity
Please keep your charity
If it comes with atrocity,
For our ability
Is in our unity,
And our prosperity
Is from divinity,
Take away your rascality
And your pomposity,
Take also your promiscuity
And your liability,
Keep them all in totality,
For our diversity
Is a property,
Our accountability
Is not divisibility,
Our generosity
And accessibility
Will not be our vulnerability,
We have the possibility
And the positivity
Backed with our deity,
That, is the suitability
And the sustainability
Not a probability,
That we abhor poverty
Will not fly our nudity
Nor take us to timidity,
We love posterity
And also dexterity
So our uniformity
Caps our integrity,
In all humility
And honesty
We go for quality
Not quantity,
So, poor obscurity
Take your severity
And leave our serenity,

That, is our security,
Gather your absurdity
And also your insanity,
Pick your enmity
We love purity,
Our sensitivity
Will decode your activity,
Our flexibility
Will detect your calamity,
With audacity
And creativity
We will avoid extremity
With so much maturity,
For this principality
Is not ambiguity,
So sovereignty
And superiority
Dare not give us obesity,
Our compatibility
And availability;
Both are a peculiarity
Buttressing the popularity
Of our formidable city,
As we ward off complexity
To restore The Dignity Of Our Identity.

HOME

Home, a gift from above
Always on the move,
With raw strength and love
But some burn it up.

Home, a place of magic
With a celestial tonic
That transcends human logic,
But some raze it down.

Home, the dwelling place of God
Built on the rock not mud,
A beautiful flowering bud
But some poke it with rod.

Home, an amazing Paradise
Always on the rise,
Helping the fool to be wise
But some turn out to be lice.

Home, a coat of every colour
Giving blessing and favour
Adding yeast and flavour
But some poison with glamour.

Home, a place of justice
Warding off every malice,
Serving all from the chalice
But some cook prejudice.

THE PROGRESSIVES WHOSE CHANGE IS RETROGRESSIVE

Dear Power, You are a tower
You hover around with a flower, like a lover
But cover the blessings that shower.

Dear Head, You are the lead
You bead the dead, to spark stampede
Then read the creed to bid well the deed.

You tie and dye
To make it a do or die.

You neither heed to the need of the seed
Nor sow to the glow of the flow,
You feed the bleed.

The anger and aggression you permit,
With danger and obsession can only limit.

Listen to the flute
It may not be so cute,
But it cannot keep mute;

Your zeal to reveal
Your bell to rebel
Your quest and request for conquest;
They all, suggest you properly digest.

Dear Power, from where did you originate
That you intoxicate,
On self, you urinate
You complicate delicate issues,
Weakening poor tissues

This race by horse and donkey
This cruise by squirrel and monkey
This struggle of time and money
This tussle for the bee and honey;
With so much energy and allergy
A concur, a murmur

29

And a liquor to stupor
A bit of surd, a bit absurd
Weird, wired, and whacky
Beware, be mindful, be watchful, be careful
Lest, you become Dear Power;
The Progressives Whose Change Is Retrogressive.

CAST AWAY THIS SPELL

If you have a brain
Wash it in the rain,
Keep it clean and plain
No matter the pain,
So that you will not complain.

Let no nonsense fill it
Otherwise you become a misfit,
Despite how you look fit.

Come out of the pit
For you to knit,
And do your bit.

If you feed a child
With something mild
Seldom will he go wild,
But if you want to drain
Allow him to stain.

Beware of every seed and grain
That you labour not in vain,
For struggle can incur loss
Even when harvest should be in gross.

Take note of goodwill
No matter the will,
Remember the highly spirited
Can also be limited
Especially when profit
Does not amount to benefit.

Now, hear the alarm
Never be fooled by charm
Lest you receive raw harm.

Hear again the bell
If you want to dwell
Cast away this spell
Lest you drown in its well.

VERDICT OF THE GODS

One hell of a muse
Picked from the refuse
Put into a special use,
To teach and confuse.

One hell of a muse
A moment with a rose
The next with ruse,
Another with a goose
The next, a runny nose
Awhile on a cruise
Next, a hard bruise.

One hell of a muse
Just like a fuse,
Interweaving poetry and prose
Interlocking a compose,
Sandwiching all in a dose.

Written on a book
Tied on a hook
Every cranny and nook,
Listen, hear, think, and look.

Hark! Put your lighters up!
Mark the door at the top
Search for peace in the dark
Go for it like a Shark.

Put your lighters up
Strike tunes and chords
Break bows and swords
Melt arrows and rods
Give hugs and nods.

Hear, you lioness
Hearken, you princess
Hasten, you goddess
Heed, you tigress
Speak to the Congress;
Announcing The Verdict Of The Gods.

PEACE IS PRICELESS

Peace is a purificator
It cures like a doctor,
Peace is a radiator
It shapes like a mentor,
Peace is a gladiator
It fights the alligator,
Peace is an agitator
It watches like a monitor,
Peace neither feels superior
Nor grows inferior.

Peace is a mirror
It cannot depict terror
If unity is the interior,
Peace is a reflector
It cannot reflect horror
When love is the exterior.

Peace is supreme
Violence is extreme,
If we cannot helm
Let us not overwhelm,
Peace is not a minor
It is everything, major.

Hence, from the anterior
To the posterior
Here is my stance;
Give peace a chance
So that we could dance
Even from a distance,

Because Peace Is Priceless.

HISTORY

History:
You have your time
Whether low or prime,
You have your lime
With or without a dime.

History:
Without a crime
You are sublime,
So you need no thyme
For you to rhyme.

History:
You make me wonder
And look yonder,
Trying to ponder
Deep through the thunder
As men do blunder
Wanting to put asunder
In a bid to plunder
And squander.

History:
Amidst the storms
You serve worms
In a calabash;
A kind of balderdash.

History:
You start an art
To fart in our heart,
You thwart the chart
And part the mart
Then, dart things apart.

History:
You hide the rears

And draw spears,
You bury Ruth
And hide the truth.

History:
On knees, bended
Sweet to the feet,
Sour, in an hour;
You are stranded.

History:
You need no spice
To thicken the dice,
But you can ginger
If you are a singer.

History:
Moulded with clay
Branded a play,
Motives on display.

History:
Loud like a barrel
Long and parallel
Like a brothel
Feeding a cartel.

History:
A lot of noise
Slow like tortoise
Afloat like porpoise,
Thorny like porcupine
Yet, speeding the turbine.

History:
Even the memory
Can fluctuate
No matter how accurate,
But distortion
Is an abortion:
It can violate

It can frustrate,
It can manipulate
And it can humiliate.

History:
Stories in a heap
Costly and cheap.

HEAVEN, I NEED A HUG.

If you stand clean
They dismantle where you lean,
If you lay low
They give you a blow,
If you fall asleep
They dig you deep,
Heaven, I need a hug.

If you are stubborn
They break your horn,
If you are childish
They make you foolish,
If you are wise
They hold you not to rise,
Heaven, I need a hug!

If you build a ladder
They squeeze your bladder,
If they make you madder
They grow gladder,
If you stay awake
They send you to the lake,
If you want to flee
They unleash thousands of bee,
Dear Heaven, give us a hug!

In the cradle
It was a puddle,
In the jungle
It was a rattle,
In the battle
It is a hurdle,
Heaven, we need a hug!

Hug our land
Rug it by your hand
Plug it to stand
Bug; may it withstand;
Heaven, hug us now!

Give us a suitor
Not a captor,
Heaven, lay siege
That none may besiege
Strengthen our handle
Lest we dwindle,
Send your dove
To renew our love
Heaven, hug us now like never before!

POETIC ABRACADABRA

When Angel Lucifer married Delilah, they bore a son named
Goliath, whose gigantism gave victory.

That, made prophetess Jezebel to seduce Bishop Nebuchadnezzar,
and gave him a son, Cain, who later built the golden calf.

And when Pontius Pilate reigned over Herod, Baal performed great
signs and wonders.

Saint Judas saved Ahab from the Eunuchs who came to rape him,
and the Chamberlains served Lazarus.

Manna fell continuously in the Garden of Eden, feeding the
Babylonians.

And Esau built the ark with his porridge and birthright.

Simeon sang the nunc dimitis to mark the beginning of the Lord's
Supper, hence John baptized Elizabeth.

So the disciples rebuked the ten plagues through Golgotha and
Calvary.

And as the foolish virgins took over the groom and guests, water
instantly turned to wine.

Then Mordecai, Joseph the Carpenter, and Apostle Harman
presented Isaac in the temple.

Furthermore, as Holy Pharaoh announced the Passover on the eighth
day of creation, the fourth God incited Socrates who instigated
Shakespeare to foretell the Armageddon.

And heaven was amazed, hitherto!!!

MY NATAL STAR

My dear natal star
Please do not go to war
Rather go into solitude
And examine your attitude,
Search well your robe
And do yourself a probe,
Interpret the novella
Tell if it means one umbrella.

My natal star
Do not cross the bar
For the long claws of fate
Have clause with date,
So if you close the gate
You may lose your mate,
However, if you retain this state
Your growth will be late.

My natal star, dear
You make me fear,
From troubles abstain
Your heritage, sustain.

Our land needs this urge
Our people deserve this passion
Our schools will thrive in this eagerness
Our hospitals will live under this enthusiasm
Our roads should have such spotlight,
But you bring home a scourge
And unleash a mission
You create uneasiness
And build antagonism,
You generate a fight
And watch your pride slip
As you captain the ship,
Dear natal star
Are you not supposed to shine?

Dear natal star
You are going too far
If you put off your torch
You will lose the couch
And end up within the porch
With no one to touch
Nor for you, vouch.

My natal star
If you break the jar
There will be no medal of honour
Nor bangle of humour,
No anklet of pride
No ring of love
No signet of power
No symbol of authority,
No clock of peace
No crown of unity
No staff of justice
No aura of friendliness,
No scarf of progress
No belt of strength
No bracelet of defence
No boot of safety
No shield of posterity,
No guard of victory
No armour of history
And above all, no coat of happiness.

Dear natal star
Be a galaxy
Rather than a shooting star,
One can gyrate in harmony
And the other, in matrimony
One can dance in symphony
And the other, in agony
One may fly in felony
The other, march in scrutiny,
One may excel in tyranny
While others succeed in mutiny,
No matter who is in custody

And the frequency of the melody,
The truth is sacred and holy;
There is no competition in destiny.

COMMON SENSE

Take this tonic
And forget the logic,
It is a magic
For the topic,
It may not be gigantic
But sure, historic
And later fantastic.

So no matter what they stole
From our hole
We can play our role
And mount the pole
To regain all in whole
And stand on our sole,
Yes, we can.

In every town, there is a lunatic
He may be dramatic
And also diplomatic,
When things seem static
He can be drastic
And question the chaotic
To flush the toxic
No matter how hectic.

We can live in peace
And not on ourselves, piss
We can have more increase
And still nothing, miss
Yes, we can
But if we freeze
We will all hiss.

You may not be an orator
To give some humor
You may not be a tutor
To be an author,
But the sculptor
And the curator
With the narrator
Are each a collaborator
And can anything censor,
Lest we drink to stupor
And empower the captor.

This is my confidence
That our competence
And affluence
Are enough defence,
Not negligence
And pretence
Because prudence
Is a complete sentence
Whether a word or tense.

And that is from my lens;
Trying to make some Common Sense.

MEN OF THE UNDERWORLD

I see footwears
They are beautiful
And sparkling,
But they step on toes
And bring woes,
Creating too many foes.

I hear footsteps
They are loud
Even in the crowd,
And they laud
Against the cloud,
They tiptoe
Even in one shoe
They have each, a hoe
Even the holy Joe.

I see footmarks
Some are big
Stinking like pig,
Some are small
Telling a fall,
They bar the wall
And seize the ball.

I see footprints
Enroute the jungle
Leading astray;
Footprints of wanderers
Fingerprints of murderers
Thumbprints of slanderers;
Traits of fate
Traces of hate.

I see footwears
Dazzling diamonds,
I hear footsteps
Bitter Almonds,
I see footmarks

Vindictive hallmarks
I see footprints:
Buried Desmonds.

They lace their footwears
And follow footsteps
Creating footmarks,
Men of the underworld
Paving footpaths
And leaving footprints
Planting feet with, and on anything,
Anytime, anywhere, and anyhow.

ESHI
We pray your reign on the throne
Be stronger than the bone,
May trouble never you, clone
Nor our land experience cyclone,
May our foundation forever be on Stone
And never again to pain, be prone
Rather all terrors and evil prune
And from horrors; away and lone
As we align in peaceful tone,
Enjoying bliss and heavenly tune
Never ever to be barren.

Happy Birthday Eshi Nkwerre,
Imenyi! Opia Egbe!

PUT YOUR HOUSE IN ORDER

You perforate your roof
And wonder why you drench,
You loosen your pillars
And doubt why you collapse,
You break your hedges
And ask why you are besieged,
You destroy your walls
And question why you are unsafe,
My people, put your house in order.

You bear a log in your eyes
And point at someone else's,
You swing like a pendulum
Yet accuse those, unstable
You are neither here nor there
Yet you list the lukewarm,
My people, put your house in order.

You can live in the moon
And still be a baboon,
You cannot be a balloon
And live inside a cocoon,
My people, put your house in order.

Put your house in order
Lest you suffer a disorder
Never allow a murder,
Because it entangles broader.

Strengthen your ladder
And focus on the radar,
Then you will be gladder
That you put your house in order.

For this war you seek
Will last longer than a week,
It will bruise your cheek
And crush the meek,
Please put your house in order
In order to maintain your border.

SUPER BAND

Come now so we can sail
Try hard that we not fail,
Hold well the sure rail
And burn open the red mail,
For us not to later wail
But rather clean our dirty tail.

Come now let us converse
Let there be a new verse
As we make a reverse
So that no matter the fierce
We can togetherly pierce,
Otherwise, all we would nurse
May just be coarse.

Listen, advise your rage
Wear it a kind courage
Be a heroic sage
And write well your page
Let it be for more than one age.

Hearken, there is a serene
It is a noble gene
Wear its godly aroma
And put it not to coma.

This soil is not a sand
It is a blessed land
Give me your lovely hand
Let us build a Super Band.

OLD SCHOOL

Our forefathers were old school
They were a people so cool
No matter how crude their tool,
They were never any fool
And their love was whiter than wool.

Our ancestors were so real
They had farms of cereal
And barns of meal,
Their peace was a deal
And their word, a seal
All that, did heal.

Our patriarchies were selfless
They were not heartless,
Their might was boundless
And their passion, so fearless
Their vision was 'painless'
And their force never lawless.

Our lineage was very strong
They never did a historic 'wrong'
Rather they wrote a heroic song
And their actions were greatly long.

Our genealogy 'was' great
They truly put in their sweat,
And they were very straight.

Our forebears were foresighted
They had common goals
And accomplished same missions,
They undertook mighty projects
And gained unique fame.

Our torchbearers were light;
Dedicated, committed and reliable
Neither mean nor cruel,
They neither threatened nor set up.

Our predecessors were mentors
They were neither traitors nor detractors.

MY DEAR NEW SCHOOL

My dear new school
  you urinate inside the pool
    to contaminate the meek
      and slay the weak.

You are too curious
  extravagant, extreme and furious
    a kiss of betrayal
      survival of the fittest.

You are wild, careless and proud
  full, cultureless and loud,
    dear new school, so impatient
      you prefer container to content.

Intolerant, reluctant and ignorant
  lubricant to unimportant mutant
    racing yet so constant
      instant, still redundant.

My dear new school
  you are such an infant
    and a poor migrant,
      so be not a militant.

You are too young
  to sound the gong
    boasting you are strong,
      o how wrong!

Go home, son, return
  never blow up your territory
    so that by the time it is your turn
      you would have learned gallantry.

THE ANSWER IS BLOWING IN THE WIND

Labour is undignifying
Hardwork is disgusting,
Bravery is belittling
Honesty is a mockery
Integrity is a loophole,
The answer is blowing in the wind.

Norms are dark, and values muddy
Morals are traps, and principles are jokes,
The answer is blowing in the wind.

Moral decadence is the anthem
Desecration is the emblem,
Abomination is the motto
Ungodliness is the logo,
The answer is blowing in the wind.

Weep for yourselves
Wail for your unborn
For civility has devoured you
And development defeated you,
But look around and see
That the answer is blowing in the wind.

This growth you chase
This foundation you lay
This culture you imbibe
This new school you embrace
And this old school you crush,
I hope you can hear the noise
Yes, the answer is blowing in the wind.

As you arouse your fantasy
And house not your embassy,
As you burn candles for dogs
And light up the gutters,
Listen and hear the shattering;
The song of the dissidents
Singing the answer is blowing in the wind.

Ride on, cheer on, pass it on
Hang in there, enjoy the bundle of lust,
However, weep for the world
For the answer would be blown away;
Away, far away from mankind.

EVEN IN OUR NEST

We can beat our chest
  to protest
   if we fail a test,
    but as a guest
     we cannot be a pest
      no matter the quest.

We must invest
  in order to manifest
   so that we can rest,
    even in the west.

Our masquerade
  must parade,
   if them, we grade
    lest we fade.

But to be made
  we must dismantle the barricade
   or expect a cascade
    even in the crusade.

When we reject
  we eject,
   when we correct
    we protect,
     when we reflect
      we perfect,
       when we deflect
        we defect,
         so when imperfect
          we invite some negative effect.

Hence when we suggest
  we hope for the best,
   as we digest
    even in our nest.

DEAR SELF

Dear self, mount the scale
And ponder anew,
Be you male
Or female.

Whether hearty and hale
Or sick and pale,
Wage the Stormy gale
Lest they tag you for sale.

Dear vision, mount the stage
With all your rage
Write the page
That would pay homage
And bring good wage.

Dear dream, do not sleep
Rather search yonder and deep,
But watch the steep
That you do not weep,
So though you creep
Or crawl and peep
Never idolize the jeep.

Dear ambition, run and push
But do not brush
Lest you crush,
Remember with rush
You can flush
Wash, whitewash and or brainwash
Our dear green bush.

Dear wish, think and grow
Plan, execute and flow
But not with a blow,
Never go low
That you tow
A forbidden row
Or uproot a divine sow

Just to glow
Or for a show.

Dear desire, keep on burning
That you may be stunning
Set yourself ablaze
And let them gaze
At the maze,
Burn, ignite, rekindle the fire
Go on, inspire
And never expire,
Let them hire
To wire.

Dear purse, stretch and expand
Never grow thin like pin
Win without the gin,
In, against sin
Do not steal the tin
That you bring no curse
Upon your course,
No matter the cause.

Ponder anew, dear self
Neither be selfish nor sheepish
Flourish, be not foolish
Polish, be not sluggish
Nourish, do not malnourish.

Dear self, ponder anew
Because it can take a few
To give the clue
That will turn the world blue
And make it permanently glue.

Help, dear self, sew
Make things new,
Spread the heavenly dew
On every pew.

Dear self, awake
Everything is at stake
Forget the sugary cake,
Never be fake
For the unborn and their sake,
Lest they drown in this mighty lake,
When necessary, apply the brake
Where important, use the rake
Remember it is a make and break
As you pray for the wake.

Now dear hope, be up and doing
As you are running
Also keep the flag flying,
For a great coming
And a glorious homecoming
That would be overwhelming.

DEAR LOCAL ASSEMBLY

Blow the bugle
And summon every eagle
Let them circle
For the battle.

Let them tackle
And dismantle
The burgle,
So that they can buckle
And suckle
Our angle.

Heal our uncle
Of his bruised ankle
That we tangle
And entangle,
Lest we disentangle
Our triangle.

Dear red cap Chambers
And distinguished members
You are the numbers
To erase our blunders.

Dear green cabinet
You wear our signet,
In a pure white singlet
You are the magnet
To attract the set
That will arrange our net.

Dear red cap
There is a gap
On the map,
It will bring a sap
If they tap
From our lap,
Wake from your nap
And do a recap

To halt the crap.

Dear green cabinet
You are the chief
To stop such grief,
Chase the thief
And quench his mischief,
Bless the leaf
To heal the deaf.

Then we would merry
With the cherry
And strawberry
Without any query
As a royal Jerry
Captains our ferry.

Dear title
Calm down, be gentle
Never belittle
Even the little,
Rather rear the cattle
With divine mantle,
And the weather
Would add a feather
To the Almighty Father.

WHAT IS WRITTEN IS WRITTEN

If you are a big brother
Mama hopes that you will provide
Papa believes you will represent,
We look up to you for example.

If you are a big brother
In any field of life,
Please stay calm and away
If you cannot be a destiny helper.

Tie us not to debtors
And scare away suitors,
Hang not around us
If you will not marry us,
Never divert attention to yourself
When we take the center stage.

Palliatives; jobless brothers
Giveaways; hungry sisters
Frustrated relatives and hopeless wards
Fame, fortune, glory and dominion.

Water me when I am burning
And fire me when I am cold,
Do not water and fire me
Like a campaign promise.

Read us not your political manifesto
Whereas you have stored up sweet potato,
And watch us rot like tomato.

Leave us to fate
If poverty has come to stay,
Allow us to debate
Hardship is a terrible way,
Do not add salt to injury.

Talents wasting, dreams dying
Visions fading, ambitions drying
Timber and caliber, merrying.

But if you are a big brother
And you cannot defend mother,
Need I be ashamed on your behalf?

If you can help
You must not be appeased,
If you can save
It must not be your child.

Sound it loud and clear
Dear conditions precedent
And conditions subsequent;
Tomorrow is a mystery.

Thank God, God is not a man,
Therefore what will be will be
Because What Is Written Is Written.

BEWARE

Beware that if pranks empty our tanks
We cannot bank on our rank,
If tricks destroy our bricks
We cannot pick them very quick,
If we make sick our chick
We will never thank what we drank.

Beware that if fraud writes on our board
We cannot hoard it in the cupboard
Lest we ring the bell of hell,
So when a house becomes a joke
It will be hard to put off the smoke,
And it will choke
Even those who poke.

Beware that we must profess
What we confess
So that as we progress
Through the process,
It will be a success.

Hence, to the shrines, and to the mountains
From the lines to the fountains,
Beware of mines, be they gold or land.

ARISE O' COMPATRIOTS

When the clouds are full
They empty 'themself' on the earth,
When the muscles pull
They challenge their health,
And when we hold the horn's bull
We click on wealth,
Arise O' Compatriots!

If our rug harbours the bug
The dog may drink from our jug
Then we may hug the grave they dug,
Arise O' Compatriots!

See, the tick is thick
And filled with blood,
The thorn is torn
And has bared the flesh,
Hear the flood
It sings afresh,
Arise O' Compatriots!

If we price nice the dice
We eat twice or thrice the rice,
Arise and shine!

Awake! Wall thy house
Prepare, ye men and mouse
Arise O' Compatriots!
Spare not even one louse
Lest vain be the labours of thy heroes' past!

SHINE YOUR LIGHT

Read beyond the line
See that all is not well
You are to make it fine
So pull down the cell,
And free your people
Lest they tumble,
Shine your light!

Sell not your hind
Tell it to the wind,
The darkness is gathering
And pythons are meandering,
Shine your light!

Shatter the ceiling
And unleash healing,
Bless the land
And let calm, stand
Shine your light
And make it bright!

Stay awake, young blood
Give strength, pure flood
Grant peace, divine Lord
Shine your light!

Sane is he who understands
Jane is she who withstands,
Fane is the lost
Cane not the dead,
Rather shine your light!

Shine your light,
Night is tight
Sight the flight,
Fight the plight.
Shine your light!

Shine it brighter
Shine it faster
Shine it, Master
Shine it against disaster!

Delight the right
For might is not right,
Light your shine
Your light; shine
Shine your light!

HAPPY FATHERS' DAY
(Dedicated To All Fathers)

My father, my teacher
My guard, my vanguard
My guardian, my custodian
My historian, my librarian
My director, my mentor
My hero, my mirror
My model, my citadel
Happy Fathers' Day, Dad.

Real, raw, natural
Brave, bold, bright
Humble, honest, hopeful
Sane, sound, strong
Blessed, gifted, talented
Disciplined, soldier, survivor
Tested and trusted,
Happy Fathers' Day, Dad

We rejoice with our Fathers
May God settle all matters,
Happy Fathers' Day!

DEAR WANDERER

Return, young wanderer
Home is cold
As you deviate bold,
Cravings can be misleading.

Come home, beloved wanderer
Home is god
Break not the rod,
Yearnings can be terminating.

Papa is at stake
Mama is awake
Kinsmen shake
Stop the home-quake,
Miseducation can cause miscarriage.

Yesterday, you misused
Today, you misbehave
Tomorrow, you will misunderstand
Come home, poor wanderer
Lest you turn a murderer.

You are not a misfit
Do not misrepresent,
You are not a mischief
Do not miscalculate,
You are not a misfortune
Do not misinform,
You are not a misplacement
Do not mistake,
You are not a misfire
Do not misconceive,
You are not a mishap
Do not misguide,
You are not a misprint
Do not misconduct,
You are not a misnomer
Do not miseducate,
You are not a misalliance

Do not misapply,
You are not a misgovernment
Do not misappropriate,
Young wanderer, darkness is not light!

You wander afar off
Without a guiding star
You cook the tar
To melt the jar
And fan a war
That will destroy the par,
Return, dearest wanderer.

The forest is thick
Loneliness will make you sick,
Be you Tom, Harry or Dick
Come home now, very quick
Hear the times tick!

THE THIRTEENTH DISCIPLE

Born not in the manger
He is not a manager,
The rocket is his pocket
He came for his name.

He is not a Jesus
He can cut off ears with scissors,
The thirteenth disciple
He is a giant not a cripple.

He is not a messenger
Neither is he a passenger,
He is not a preacher
Nor is he a teacher.

The thirteenth disciple
Biting mama's nipple
Putting her in tension
With an intention.

On ascension, Jesus ascended
And promised us the comforter,
For detention, this one descended
And unleashed the defaulter.

He is not the Saviour
He does not have the flavour,
Even with his convoy
He is not an envoy,
He can be an astronaut
But not a diplomat,
The thirteenth disciple
Bible is not his apple.

On the seventh day, God rested
For compassion is His thirst,
On the eighth day, man tested
For senseless is his taste.

Are you a thirteenth disciple,
Did Jesus call you?
Are you the thirteenth disciple
Did you call yourself?

ONE BIG FAMILY

Beautiful like the lily
Flowing in glory,
We are one big family.

Old and young
Bold and strong
Male and female
Hale with tale,
We are one big family.

We are one big tree
Lovely, great and free
We are honey, we are bee
We find some glee,
Even in steel.

We are one big umbrella
We are not the gorilla
Rather we are the guerrilla,
And we have our Stella.

This family can survive the stitch
And scale any ditch,
One big family through the storm
One big family, we always perform.

NEW DAWN

It is a new dawn
Let us ponder anew
As we play in the lawn
With our crew.

It is a new dawn
And there is a long way to go
We need not be withdrawn,
Let no one say no.

It is a new dawn
The collage can be drawn
The mosaic can be felt,
If we tighten our belt.

It is a new dawn
Leave no good undone
So that we can fly,
And never cry.

A dawn so new and fresh
A new way of thinking
To avert a huge sinking,
A war against our flesh
Please fight without blinking
For us to win without shrinking.

Yes, it is a new dawn
Put on the armour of God
Let's cast away our pod
And let blossom our bud.

LIFE IS A MYSTERY

Life is a mystery
It can cook penury
And serve misery,
It does not matter our holiness.

Life is a mystery
It can buy us toy
And bring joy,
It does not matter our ugliness.

Life is a lane
It can make us sane
And still crash our plane,
It cares not our gentleness.

Life is a steep
It can hurt us deep
And make us weep,
It bothers, not our success.

Life is a surprise
It can cause sunrise
And make us wise,
It questions not our stupidity.

Life is a mirror
It can reflect our error
And unleash on us, some horror
It matters not our carefulness.

Life is a challenge
It can cut off the edge
And quake our hedge,
It fears not our sanity.

Life is a game
It does not ask our name
Nor respect our fame,
It can serve us absurdity.

Life is a gift
It can be swift
It can lift
It can shift,
It can sadly drift.

Life is a coupon
Sour like lemon
Dangerous like demon,
It hears not the sermon.

Life is a luck
It gives no damn the lock,
It can crush like block
And harden, like rock
Leaving a great shock.

Life is changeful
For those who mock;
The pig becomes a pork,
Nobody knows what is in stock.

Life is vast
High like mast
Present and past
Future and last.

IN THE WINGS OF THE SUN

Now, it heavily rains
Sweeping away our gains
Making noisier the chains
But it will wash off our stains.

Now we drench and shiver
We cannot perch or ginger
And we cannot use our quiver,
But we will fly around the globe.

In the wings of the sun
We shall fly and run
To merry and have fun,
Never to bind our nun.

See, the rays appear
Spreading far and near
Cry not nor fear
For they are rays of hope.

In the wings of the sun
We shall dry the earth
And have pure breath
Smiling up to heaven
Breaking even the proven,
It will not be a pun.

In the wings of the sun
We shall gather soon,
To play under the moon
No matter how fierce the noon.

In the wings of the sun
We shall dance round the world
Holding firm our sword
To cut off every discord.

In the wings of the sun
We shall always twinkle
And never break an ankle.

In the wings of the sun
We shall again sparkle,
To heat up the waves
And warm our caves.

In the wings of the sun
We shall embrace brotherhood
And rekindle our values,
We shall anoint the neighborhood
And take off to the blues.

In the wings of the sun
We shall smile down
Looking at our town,
How beautiful her wedding gown.

In the wings of the sun
We shall fight all obstacles
Though they tower like pinnacles,
They shall turn into miracles.

Then we shall sing and dance
How we crushed the nuisance
And turned the circumstance;
Into a soulful nuance.

On the wings of the sun
We shall fly like birds
And soar like eagles.

Under the wings of the sun
We shall hotly blaze
For the world to gaze
And get lost; amazed.

CONQUER THE WORLD

When woken by trouble
Shoot it more than double,
When dared by thorns
Raise and protect your horns,
Go, conquer the world.

When stuck in the jungle
Increase the tempo of the struggle,
For as a Knight in shining armour
Your strength is more than a glamour.

Go, conquer the world
Lord and rule the rings
Spread forth your wings
Fasten all your swings,
And surprise the kings.

There will be a famine
There will be a roadblock
They will tend to undermine
But fail not to graze your flock.

Hold on to your goal
Burn it up like coal,
Your passion will bear you witness
Even if you made no success.

Try harder, you will win
You will never be in the bin,
Though as small as pin.

Conquer the world, I say
Go all out, it will pay
It may not be money
But sure, sweeter than honey.

Look, the furrow is narrow
So follow too, your marrow
The hollow you need not borrow

Lest sorrow scatter all you sow
Focus on the row, though it be low
For then you will conquer the world.

The world, we need conquer
The mysteries we must ponder
Hear now the rumbling thunder
Gently whispering 'look yonder'

CALM DOWN

Calm down, brethren
Bless, do not curse
Give from your purse
At the Lord's impulse.

Calm down, beloved
Relax, do not be angry
Lest we exceed the boundary.

Honourable Nkwerre, It's okay
Off your anger, off your anger
Calm down, relax brethren.

Rivalry undermines chivalry
Manipulation stains ordination
Envy unleashes the bevy,
Calm down, brothers and sisters.

Until we calm down
We may continue to drown
Because a restless town
Will always have to frown.

Relax, calm down, brethren
Children, women and men,
For us to produce fertile semen.

Calm down, the land is pure
Relax, be safe and sure
For there is only a divine cure
Let not selfishness lure.

We are one people
Give peace one last chance,
Wipe your tears, wipe your tears
Off your anger, Honourable Nkwerre
It's okay, it's okay
Mummy, calm down.

Included on the cover of this great book "DEAR NKWERRE" are the barges of the ancient schools in Nkwerre. They are:

St Catharine's Girls' Secondary School, Nkwerre. (The author's alma mater)

Motto: FROM STRENGTH TO STRENGTH

St Augustine's Grammar School, Nkwerre.

Motto: IBU ANYI DANDA

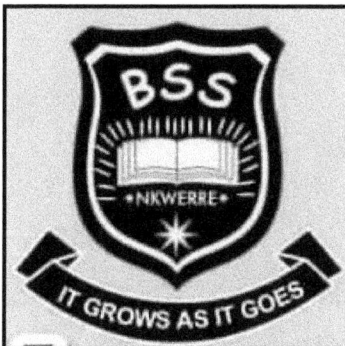

Boys' Secondary School, Nkwerre.

Motto: IT GROWS AS IT GOES

These three schools were the three oldest secondary schools in my hometown, Nkwerre. Students from Nigeria and outside Nigeria, especially neighbouring countries like Cameroon, Gabon, etc, schooled in them. They would remain green and evergreen to their old boys and girls, irrespective of CHANGE.

The crossed guns above the elephant signifies the Nkwerre people's craft, and what they were and are known for in the olden days.

Nkwerre people dealt in gun carving and gun production until the arrival of the white man. They were a people that loved blacksmith. The elephant signifies pride, strength, unity, vigour, vitality, peace, beauty, power, and excellence.

Till date, they answer and respond to IMENYI! OPIA EGBE!! as greeting, exclamation, identity, identification, jubilation, celebration, ...

ABOUT THE AUTHOR

Ngozi Olivia Osuoha is a Nigerian poet/writer/thinker, a graduate of Estate Management with experience in Banking and Broadcasting.

She has featured in over seventy international anthologies and has also published over two hundred and sixty poems in over twenty five countries.

She has authored twenty two poetry books, and some of her poems have been translated and published into some languages including Polish, Spanish, Russian, Romanian, Farsi, Arabic, Khloe, Macedonian, among others.

She has won several awards and some of her poems have been nominated for the Pushcart Prize and Best Of The Net Awards.

She has numerous words on marble. She is also a tailor.

www.ingramcontent.com/pod-product-compliance
Lightning Source LLC
Chambersburg PA
CBHW071841020426
42331CB00007B/1813